A Family in Review: Reflections over the years a growing process by Evelyn Ayum

2016

WE are FAMILY

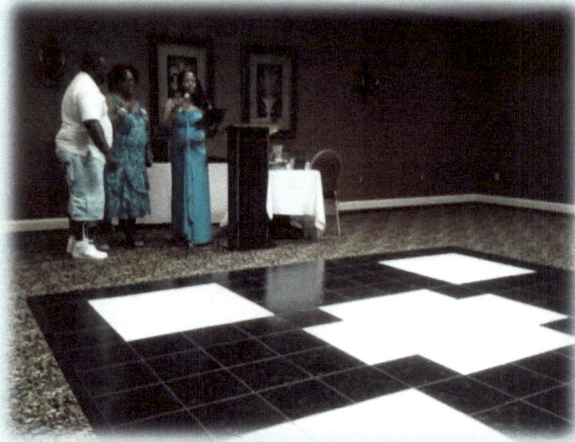

FAMILY REUNION

Our Family Reunion

FAMILY REUNION

Family Reunion

Family

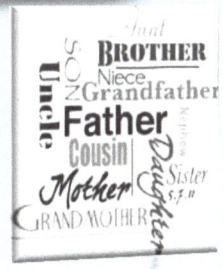

like branches on a tree,
we all grow in different directions,
yet our roots remain as one.

Aunt
BROTHER
SON Niece Grandfather
Uncle
Father
Cousin Daughter
Mother Sister 5.5"
GRANDMOTHER

Family
like *branches* on a tree,
we all *grow* in different
directions, yet our *roots remain* as one

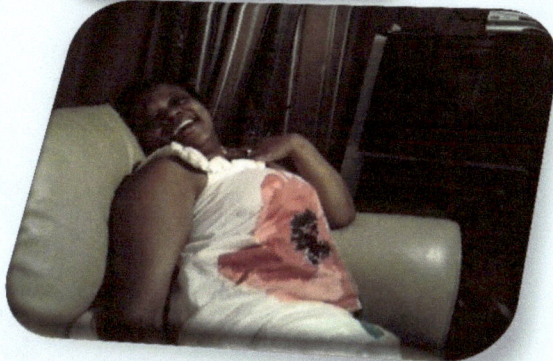

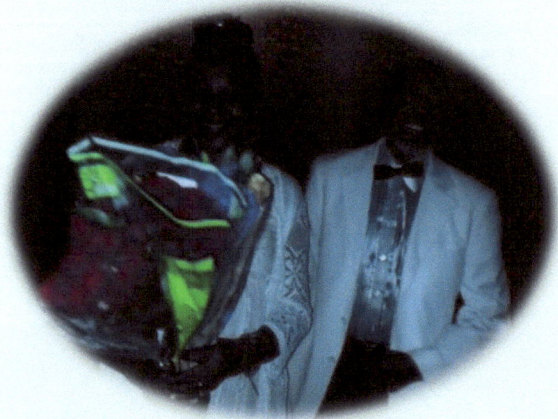

36

Our Family Reunion

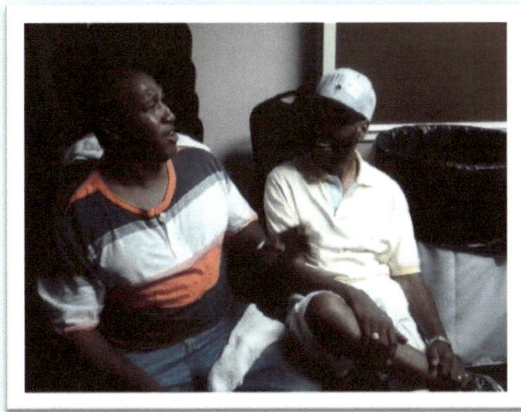

Pausing to remember...

79

"My husband, friend, mother and father."

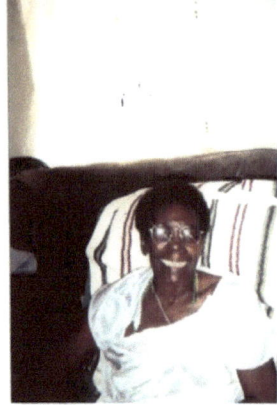

Without family where would we be...